W9-AVT-255

ABANDONED AUTOS

ISBN 0-917808-36-3
Library of Congress Card Number: 99-66950

Editor-In-Chief
Terry Ehrich

Captions
Richard A. Lentinello

Contributing Editors
Dave Brownell
Doug Damerst
Richard A. Lentinello

Designer
Rob Randall

Contributing Designers
Ed Heys
Nancy Bianco

Special thanks to
Bob Johnson Auto Literature Archives
McBride Auto Ads
McLellan's Automotive History
O'Brien's Auto Ads
for providing the old ads and
sales literature pictured within this book

Second printing, May 2000

PRINTED IN THE USA

Hemmings Motor News

ABANDONED AUTOS

An America-wide Appreciation of Aesthetically Abandoned Ancient Almost All-American Automobiles,* Artfully Assembled (and Alliteratively Annotated) for the Astute Automotive Aficionado

* a few old trucks, too, plus an Alfa Romeo, an Austin Atlantic, a De Tomaso Pantera, a Fiat, a Jaguar, a Mercedes, a Metropolitan, a Porsche, a Saab, a Simca, and four vintage Volkswagens,

The winter of 1989-90 was typical for Vermont – short cold dark days, long cold dark nights, and by mid-February you might wonder whether spring would ever come again – but it was brightened by an unexpected call from a photographer in Maine, a realtor by trade who (like any good realtor) always carried a camera in case of need to photograph new listings.

Nancy Rhey was her name, and in the course of her real estate business travels she'd noticed some of Maine's semi-forgotten treasures: abandoned cars and trucks which had begun to blend with their surroundings in ways which made them look more like jewels "in the rust" than like the junk which Lady Bird Johnson might have labeled them. Ms. Rhey began grabbing shots of these scenically situated rusty relics and had amassed an impressive portfolio worthy, she hoped, of publication.

Hemmings Motor News, by happy coincidence, had been looking for Ms. Rhey's work for some few years – we just didn't know it until we saw it! Various other publishers to the antique auto hobby had been producing old car calendars – of shiny show cars without exception – for years, and we, for years, had been looking for a way to develop a calendar which would be different, or better, or in some way distinctly recognizable as coming from *Hemmings Motor News* – a publication which had always marched (even if slightly out of step) to the beat of a decidedly different drummer.

And so was born the 1991 *Hemmings Motor News Calendar of Aesthetically Abandoned Ancient American Automobiles*. We sent it to press, and to market, hoping to sell a couple of thousand copies – we sold several thousand, and in the years since, this publishing oddity (we challenge you to show us another like it) has become one of the best selling calendars we know of, regularly selling four to five times as many copies as are sold of the more usual automotive calendar. To call it a cult item would not stretch the truth to the breaking point – we often hear from customers who have complete collections of our Abandoned Autos Calendars from the very first edition – and because each year's Calendar uses anywhere from 24 to 36 photos (each month shows a feature photo large, plus one or two smaller secondary photos) our need for fresh material has led to the establishment of *HMN's* Annual Abandoned Autos Photo Contest in which readers from around the nation and beyond send us from 800 to over a thousand photos, candidates for next year's Annual Appreciation of Artfully Assembled Aesthetically Abandoned Ancient American Automobiles (often) Alliteratively Annotated for the Astute Automotive Aficionado. From housewives and tourists to professional photographers, over 140 people from Maine to Hawaii, and foreign ports of call, have seen their work in print, and their names in lights, or at least in eight point type, as *HMN* Calendar Photo Contest winners.

Like anything healthy, these *HMN* calendars have evolved over the years. As time went along we added and modified features of the calendar so that now (1999 as this is written) our calendars are much more than just a platter of pretty photographs. We list nearly 200 important collector car show dates each year, and indicate which shows will be attended by *HMN* representatives. We include an ever-growing list of significant dates in automotive history (Louis Chevrolet's and Henry Ford's birth dates, and the date of enactment of the nation's first speed limit law, for examples), odd & interesting holidays in other lands (like Bean Throwing Day in Japan), and much more. Each year's issue can honestly be said to be an education and each has been a wonderful experience for all of us – photo contest winners and *HMN* staffers alike.

We're happy to share a sampling of nearly ten years' worth of phenomenal photos with readers of this book, and we hope you'll enjoy our variation on the old car hobby's traditional "before & after" picture theme – instead of ratty "before" snapshots of rusty dusty derelict cars or trucks and trophy-winning-restoration "after" portraits, we're using ads and sales literature for the vehicles when they were new for "before" views alongside the present-day realities of the "after" scenes captured by our intrepid roving photographers.

Terry Ehrich, Publisher
Hemmings Motor News

PS – Readers who wish to see the calendars from which these photos were selected or to purchase future years' calendars can call 1-800-CAR-HERE (extension 550). Readers with photos we should consider for future calendars should mail them to HMN Calendar Photo Contest, Att'n Rob Randall, PO Box 256, Bennington, Vermont 05201. Photos to be returned should be accompanied by self addressed stamped envelopes.

McBride Auto Ads, *Saturday Evening Post*

1956 Chrysler
Ice cold temperatures, heavy snow, and a fallen tree have been just a little too much to bear for the once majestic Chrysler at left. Showing the consequences of such indignities, it remains frozen on this central Minnesota farm under the watchful eyes of some friendly cows. Clearly, "The Year-Ahead Car" is at least a couple of light-years away from having its 225-horsepower V8 producing power in style once more.

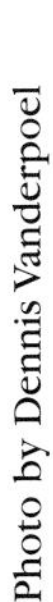
Photo by Dennis Vanderpoel

Photo by Wayne Kilpatrick

Bob Johnson's Auto Literature Archives

1936 Hupmobile
Suffering severe glaucoma of the windshield, this once-proud Hupmobile finds the thick woods of Connecticut a perfect refuge in which to wither away into oblivion. Though its unique grille and distinctive side-vent trim are long gone, a thorough restoration remains very possible judging by its intact body. The rarity of this four-door sedan, due to a temporary production stoppage in 1936-37, is another reason a Hupmobile enthusiast might undertake its rebuild.

Bob Johnson's Auto Literature Archives

Photo by Tom Narwid ©

McBride Auto Ads

1947 Buick

Entertaining thoughts of restoring this post-war Buick? Take a cue from these disheveled lines . . . run! Perhaps it hasn't reached the point of no return, but it would require several new body panels, along with a deep bank account to re-plate those acres of chrome. And considering its extended exposure in a northwestern Vermont field, lots of welding will be needed, too. But it could be worth it once that Fireball engine is re-ignited for the first time.

1950 Austin Atlantic

Thanks to its maker's judicious use of aluminum body panels, Mother Nature hasn't taken its toll just yet on this charming, streamlined Austin Atlantic A90 sitting outside a barn in South Dakota. Carefully crafted in England using the finest British parts, such as SU carburetors and Lucas "Prince of Darkness" electrics, it remains a testimony to America's misunderstanding of unconventional automobiles with oddball styling and little four-cylinder engines with fun-to-tune twin SUs.

Photo by James D. Lusk

McBride Auto Ads.

1962 Rambler
A far cry from the ad's adventurous copy—Play in it, Nap in it, Sleep in it—describing the adventure of owning this particular Rambler station wagon today, one would have to say—Scrub it, Weld it, Paint it! Due to its abandonment in the perpetually wet woods of Washington state's San Juan Island, moss has radically transformed this American Motors "vacation machine" into a two-tone green hulk of disfigured metal. We just hope the seats are down so resident critters can nap in comfort.

Photo by J. M. Vinson

Photo by Robert Harmon

McBride Auto Ads.

1953 Chevrolet Bel Air
Sleep cheap! That's exactly what many motivated masculine miners did when they took advantage of the Bel Air's spacious seats to sleep the nights away after spending laborious days extracting uranium from a cozy Colorado mine. Having stood up well to years of abuse, its rust-free shell would make it an easy car to restore. And just think of all the attention you'll get with its "glow-in-the-dark" body work.

Everyone we asked for an ad for a '41 Chevy panel truck said the same thing: "Good luck!"

1941 Chevrolet Panel Truck
The victim of another botched restoration attempt, one of Chevrolet's finest pre-war panel trucks, a 1941, now decomposes into the earth of a north central Minnesota hillside. Apart from its nicely sculptured grille, chrome adornment was strictly limited due to the insufficient supply of chrome during the immediate-pre-Pearl Harbor period. Floor mats were also eliminated during that period, which means this truck's floor is most probably well worn and very dirty.

Photo by Larry Kytola

Photo by B.J. Donnelly

McBride Auto Ads.

1936 Cord
After experiencing problems in the heat of Utah's western desert, Junior's confidence in his stylish Cord wasn't as strong as his dad led him to believe it would be. So he dumped it. Today, it would take a truly skilled fabricator, with a life-span of free time, to attempt a restoration on this badly crumpled piece of thirties Americana. But the wipers and rear windows are still in place, and that's as good a reason to start the rebuild as any, especially considering Cord's low production total of only 1,764 cars in 1936.

Maybe it's the answer for you

HERE'S a smart, moneysaving solution to the dual transportation problem on many farms—this handsome, sturdy GMC Suburban.*

On weekdays—with the rear seats slid out—it's a rugged farm truck, ready to haul crates, sacks, boxes and general cargo. On Sundays and holidays it becomes a trim highway traveler with enough seats to carry even families of eight or nine to church and town in comfort.

Remember, it's a GMC—with all *that* means in solid construction, long life and dependable, steady power—with low upkeep. Its low price will surprise you. Get the full story from your nearest GMC dealer.

*Also available in lift-and-hinged tail gate model.

GMC
GASOLINE & DIESEL TRUCKS
½ TO 35 TONS

GMC Truck & Coach Division of General Motors

O'Brien's Auto Ads, *Farm Journal*

Photo by Cat McKeen

1952 GMC Panel Truck
Highly coveted by hot rodders and custom truck builders everywhere, the ruggedly handsome GMC panel truck at right hides from the customizer's torch behind a thick patch of colorful fireweed flowers in southern Alaska. It's a little down on its luck, but its missing windows, interior and assorted trim can be easily replaced, while its durable straight-six engine might only need some fresh gas and a valve adjustment. It might, indeed, be just the answer for you!

"They're the talk of the coffee stops!"

CHEVROLET TRUCKS
FOR TRANSPORTATION UNLIMITED

O'Brien's Auto Ads, *Saturday Evening Post*

1946 Chevrolet Truck
This idyllic picture-postcard scene in northern Idaho makes a perfect setting in which this 1946 Chevrolet truck rests its weary bolts. Its green and black paint scheme helps it blend into the tall grass, thus camouflaging it from rifle-toting cowboys. With a makeshift wooden flat-bed, perhaps it was once used to haul logs down to the sawmill, which would have been an easy task for its strong 235-cubic-inch straight-six engine.

FOR SALE

Photo by Sandy Roca

1949 Seagrave Aerial Ladder Truck
Left to fend for itself in a damp field in central Massachusetts, this classic looking Seagrave ladder truck is now enjoying quieter, cooler times.
No longer rushing to the call of flaming duty, it sits by its lonesome self, waiting to be rescued so it can be restored for some light-duty action, such as parades and local shows. Appearing fairly complete with most of its accessories in place, all it's really missing is a happy little Dalmatian to keep it company.

Photo by Larry Bogel

Mcbride Auto Ads

1954 Kaiser and 1932 Chevrolet
From beauty queen to ugly duckling this is what years of unprotected exposure to the salt air can do to your car's finish, even when that seaside location happens to be on the beautiful Hawaiian island of Maui. This unlikely pairing of collectible classics is as diverse as one is likely to find: Pre-war, post-war; mass appeal, limited appeal; traditional styling, bizarre styling; all rust, no rust; windows out, windows up. Sadly, their one commonality is that they both appear currently unloved.

Photo by Daniel W. Wesen

1951 Studebaker
Stripped of its usable parts, this once spectacular Studebaker no longer commands the same attention it did back when it was a fully functional jet-streamed powerhouse on wheels. Instead of providing today's Studebaker enthusiasts with a 120-horsepower driving thrill, it sits unwanted against sagebrush at the bottom of a mountainous ravine in the colorful Colorado hills. Judging by its solid, rust-free shell, it remains a stand-out in quality.

New driving thrill! 120-horsepower wonder car!

Spectacular Studebaker Commander V-8

A jet-streamed powerhouse on wheels!
New-type high efficiency valve-in-head V-8 engine!
Sensational acceleration! Exceptional thrift!
A stand-out in quality! A bargain buy!

McBride Auto Ads, *Saturday Evening Post*

ALL-TRUCK and Loaded With Power

INTERNATIONAL Trucks

McBride Auto Ads, *Saturday Evening Post*

1947 International
After spending a laborious life hauling goods through the tough streets of Gotham City, when it came time to retire, the quietness of the rural central Ohio countryside became quite appealing to the ruggedly handsome International KB pickup at right. Looking very complete and easy to restore, this classic pickup appears to be one which can be rebuilt and driven with pride for years to come.

Photo by Jim Rogers

AP 216

PARKING

Photo by Roger W. Gardner

October, 1930 THE COUNTRY GENTLEMAN

Saying Great Things of Hudson

Records Confirm All the Praises of Owners

"I have owned seven great Hudsons—and now the Straight Eight—easily the greatest." . . . *from owner letter.*

"It is the greatest of seventeen successive Hudsons I have owned and driven." . . . *from owner letter.*

"Hudson's Great Eight is the finest of fifteen splendid Hudsons I have owned." . . . *from owner letter.*

"In owning five Hudson cars I have thought each better than the one before. But my pleasure in the Hudson Eight—in its good looks, beautiful performance and economy—convinces me this is the finest Hudson and greatest value of all." . . . *from owner letter.*

"After making over 400,000 miles on three previous Hudson cars, without any break-downs, I was convinced I could get nothing better than another Hudson. The running of my Hudson Eight is as smooth as any car twice the price." . . . *from owner letter.*

Because of the fine things owners are saying—and its pre-eminent records here and abroad—Hudson's Great Eight in its first six months became the world's largest selling Eight.*

With a perfect score it won the celebrated 9-day Tour de France against 87 cars from every country.

With perfect scores, three Hudson Eights finished equal first in the International 8-day Reliability Trial, sponsored by Poland, against the largest field ever entered.

With perfect score, against nearly all makes, it overwhelmingly won in tests conducted in the purchase of cars by the State of California.

Twenty-five Hudson Eights in 7-day non-stop motor runs totaled 124,750 miles without a mechanical failure.

One ride will reveal to you why every owner praises it—why every test gives it first place—why it became in its first six months the world's largest selling Eight.

*Official Registrations from every State in the United States

McBride Auto Ads, *The Country*

1930 Hudson Eight
As the spray paint sign suggests, this obedient touring sedan basks in the sun alongside a barn in southeastern Indiana. It's still in fine, restorable condition considering its seventy-year-old state of health, and former Hudson-owning townfolks have many great things to say about it. From its fine, understated styling and distinctive wood wheels to its smooth-running 80-horsepower straight-eight, records confirm all the praises of owners–just try to find them.

Photo by Marianne Larsen

The car that dared to be different!

1941 MERCURY 8

THE BIG CAR THAT STANDS ALONE IN ECONOMY

McBride Auto Ads

1941 Mercury
Truth in advertising finally rings true in this photograph of a dignified Mercury 8, which stands alone on a desolate prairie in South Dakota. Looking remarkably complete with all its trim attached, and with a straight, rust-free body to boot, this dare-to-be-different Merc is one abandoned automobile that wouldn't require much to get it cruising the plains once more. And with a 240-cubic-inch V8 under the hood, just think of the possibilities.

McLellan's Automotive History

1948 Hudson Pickup
"Ya can't get theyah from heeah," shouted the old timer in Maine to the young whippersnapper driver who thought he knew better. So into the woods he drove . . . and in the woods he stuck. Though this handsome Hudson truck was left for dead, its tough construction has afforded it the opportunity to survive well beyond its intended years. Even its light blue paint has held up well. The missing grille is now probably part of someone's automobilia collection.

Photo by Duane F. Boone

Photo by Richard O. Moldovan Sr.

McBride Auto Ads

Three Volkswagens
Somewhere in the great expanse of northern Illinois, lies this Old Volks Home for bedraggled Bugs and Beetles. No longer able to contribute reliable transportation service for Americans on the move, these two Beetles and a Karmann-Ghia peacefully rest their air-cooled hearts until their mechanical organs can be donated so other vintage VWs may flower into beauty once more. Remember . . . think small!

Bob Johnson's Auto Literature Archives

1949 Packard Hearse
After a career of transporting terminally quiet humans in style, as they head towards that giant retirement community underground, rigor mortis has finally set in for this once-prestigious Packard hearse. Showing few battle scars, and very few missing parts, it remains in restorable condition at its serene resting spot amid young sumacs in an Ontario, Canada clearing. Utilizing a heavy-duty long-wheelbase chassis, these workhorses rode very smoothly; just ask the man who had his final ride in one.

Photo by Harold Howe

Photo by Dennis M. Sokol

McBride Auto Ads, *Holiday*

1954 Lincoln and 1918 Fordson Tractor
Deep in the heart of a central Massachusetts forest rest these Dearborn distant cousins, each representing a distinct era of America's transportation ingenuity. While the tractor may have seen its better days already plowed under, the Lincoln has plenty of life remaining thanks to its strong build quality. And with a powerful V8 under the hood, it's no wonder this very good looking automobile won the rugged Mexican Pan-American Road Race two years in a row in 1952 and 1953.

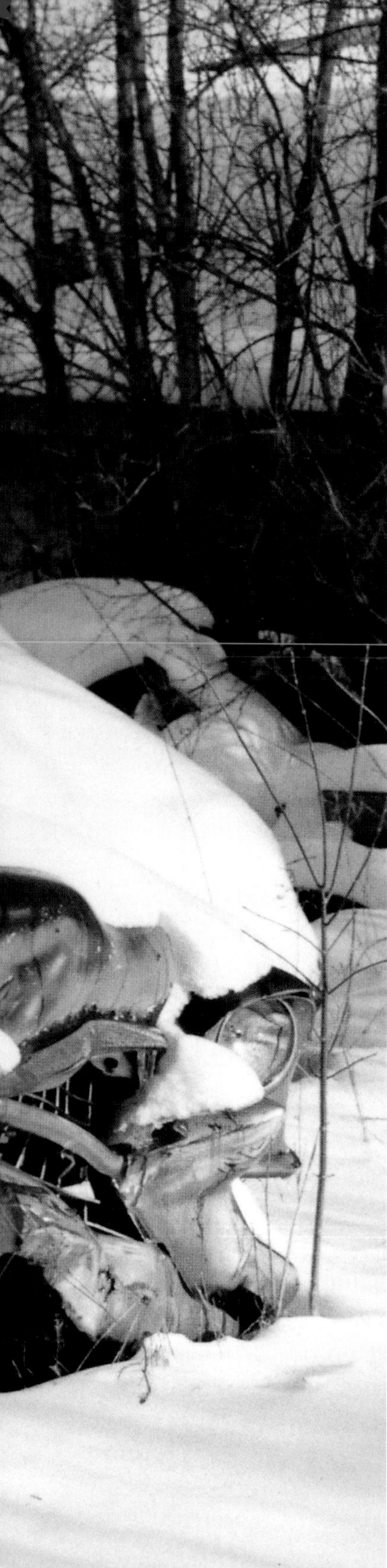

Photo by Zander Livingston

We couldn't find any promotion for Cadillac Ambulances, can you?

1955 Cadillac Ambulance
Lying in a coma due to severe trauma to its face, this disfigured Cadillac ambulance waits for some much needed surgery, frozen in a yard somewhere in central Vermont. Heavy snow covers its skin like a band-aid until it can be resprayed rescue red. With an obese-looking body featuring several hand-crafted panels, this is one professional vehicle that sorely needs some professional care. Let's hope its insurance card hasn't expired.

Photo by Zander Livingston

McBride Auto Ads.

1952 Pontiac DeLuxe Convertible
A cold, windswept field in northern Vermont is the scene for this Tin Indian's last attempt at effective internal combustion and its subsequent battle with external oxidation. Battered into submission by heavy snows, thanks, in part, to the failure of the last owner to put up the top, it is slowly melting—and sinking—into a dysfunctional heap of once-proud Poncho iron. Originally available with either a straight-six or straight-eight, it would take the power of an F-16 to pull it out of this mess.

Plymouth

Plymouth pickup promotion materials seem to have been rare to non-existant. Anybody out there got an ad or sales brochure for anticipated reprints of this book?

1938 Plymouth
Sitting on the dock of the bay, this pre-war pickup's weight proved just a tad too much for the waterlogged wood. As it continues to cool its heels in this central Florida lake, its lower-than-sea-level condition has begun to wreak havoc on its susceptible shapely coach-work, not to mention its water-filled straight-six. Now it's little more than a sandblaster's dream come true.

Photo by Harold W. Perry

Photo by Duncan Urquhart

EXCITEMENT RIDES WITH YOU *every mile you roll in your new* CHEVROLET. *At rest or on the road, this sleek style-setter promises you more go, gaiety and glamor—and you'll find it keeps its promises beautifully. Come aboard and take the key to the happiest traveling on the highway!*

McBride Auto Ads, *Newsweek*

1958 Chevrolet
You have to wonder how this Chevy ever became a structural part of the banks of the James River in Virginia. Was it driven here by pranksters? ("Drove my Chevy into the levee...") Swept away in a flood, only to fetch up in the mud like a castaway? Or did some cause more sinister place it in this watery resting place? We'll likely never know, but it is a strange and prophetic irony that the ad at left would place a 1958 Chevrolet in such close proximity to water . . . .

Bob Johnson's Auto Literature Archives

Photo by William Magers

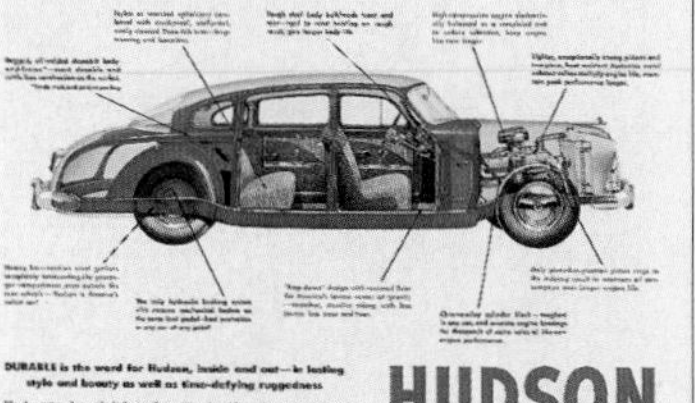

McBride Auto Ads

1951 Hudson Hornet
The durability of a Hudson automobile is legendary, as witnessed by this fairly decent looking Hornet that's been parked in the woods of central Indiana for a few too many years. With an all-welded Monobilt body and frame, chrome-alloy cylinder block and crack-proof Dura-fab trim, it remains in restorable condition, a testimony to the Hudson engineers' quest for quality. Clearly the best buy for the long tomorrow.

1942 Ford Coupe
Show up in your driveway with this worn and battered pre-war Ford and your family won't welcome you – they'll disown you. In fact, they'll probably run away when they see all the work that's needed to put this ratty-looking coupe back in shape. But first that fast-growing grove of red maples, located somewhere in central Connecticut, has to be chopped down to get at the old 90-horsepower V8 Ford. We think it's worth it.

Photo by Jeffrey T Lenak

We couldn't find an
ad for this darned Dodge.
Bet you can't either.

1933 Dodge Bus
School's out for good for this pre-war Dodge bus, now languishing behind a building somewhere in south central Montana. But in spite having suffered years of non-stop abuse at the hands of over-active school kids, some tender loving care, a couple of wheels, windows, seats, and a few gallons of fresh bright yellow paint are all this admirable school bus needs to lovingly serve its community once again.

Photo by Daniel Wesen

Photo by Aaron Huffnagle

THE COUNTRY GENTLEMAN

When Buying the Best Saves You Money

why own a lesser car?

The NEW ESSEX Challenger

McBride Auto Ads, *The Country Gentleman*

1930 Essex
Why own a lesser car? Well, if a car without windows, an engine and transmission, headlights, seats, and a few other minor incidentals like wheels and tires and a uniform paint finish appeals to you, then this classy Essex is the automobile you've been looking for. To find it, all you need to do is roam the woods of central Minnesota, preferably before the snows come, and it's yours. But if you want to save money, go elsewhere.

Photo by Robert Drake

McBride Auto Ads, *Saturday Evening Post*

1950 Ford
The "Magic Action" of Ford's king-size brakes just didn't provide enough stopping power to prevent this once fine freezing forlorn Ford four-door from falling down the hill. Thankfully its "Lifeguard" body saved enough of its life to provide a solid foundation for the next friendly fanatical Ford enthusiast to start its restoration. As it awaits its prince in these California hills, even covered with snow, its fine styling still shows through.

Photo by Peter J. Edinburg

McBride Auto Ads, *Saturday Evening Post*

1960 Chevrolet Corvair
Restoration of this stylish Monza coupe, abandoned in America's first state, Delaware, would no doubt be an ambitious undertaking. As a former *Motor Trend* "Car of the Year" star in 1960, its present condition isn't too bad for an enthusiast handy enough to bring its responsive horizontally opposed six back to life.

Photo by Colleen Hesson

McBride Auto Ads, *Country Gentleman*

1946 and 1947 Chevrolets
Former masters of style, these patriotic Chevrolet Stylemasters are now denizens of decay.
As they sit abandoned on the crest of a hill in scenic central Idaho, their days as kings of the low-cost performers are rapidly receding. Yet, more than a half-century ago, they were very popular, due to their impressive notchback styling, cavernous interiors and reliable valve-in-head 90-horsepower straight-six engines.

Photo by Jim Howe

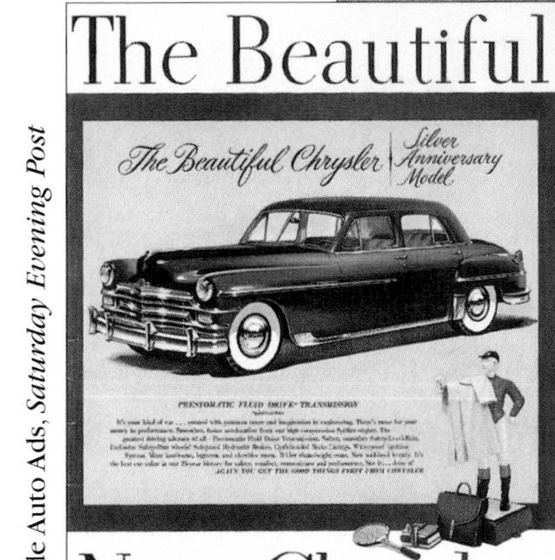

McBride Auto Ads, *Saturday Evening Post*

1949 Chrysler Coupe
The quiet, pristine wilderness of northwestern Washington state makes a relaxing backdrop for one of the most attractive post-war Chryslers ever built: the '41 club coupe. Although it's a little down at its heels, a couple of months worth of non-stop media blasting just might do the trick in de-rusting the shapely steel bodywork so paint will adhere again. But is the 135-horsepower straight-eight in any condition to out-run the white-faced bull in the background?

McBride Auto Ads

1963 Pontiac
Who needed a hobby when you could wide-track down to the country club in your stylish Bonneville and be the envy of everyone? After all, what other car sported distinctive eight-lug wheels, handsome hardtop styling, a wide-track suspension, and a big 389-cubic-inch V8 pushing out 235 horsepower? We hope, this big old Poncho resting in a back yard in Maryland will be rescued soon, so its new owner can drop his other hobbies and look cool instead.

Photo by James King

Photo by G.Alan Nelson

LET ANY DODGE DEALER TELL YOU HOW YOU CAN

Switch to Dodge and Save Money!

He has the facts in his possession.. It will be simple for him to show you how you can switch to Dodge and actually save money!

Switch TO THE BIG NEW 1937 DODGE – and Save Money!

McBride Auto Ads, *Saturday Evening Post*

1937 Dodge
Alongside an aesthetically abandoned ancient American farmhouse on a Minnesota farm, lies this decrepit four-door Dodge sedan. Reduced to a shell of its former self due to excessive exposure to the endlessly evil elements of the north, its condition is horrifying. Since it packed a mighty straight-six under the hood, no wonder many car buyers switched to Dodge back in the thirties. And with prices starting at a mere $640, big savings were had by all.

Bob Johnson's Auto Literature Archives

1953 Buick
With its big, glimmering toothy grin starting to show signs of life, this big, old Buick slowly deteriorates into the moist ground somewhere along the northern coast of Washington State. Showing very little rust amid acres of clean, straight sheetmetal, this car's renewed career cruising the drive-ins is all but five or six gallons of paint away. Not to mention four new tires and a precision tune-up for its 164-horsepower V8.

Photo by Edgar P. Boslough

Photo by Edward Burchard

Bob Johnson's Auto Literature Archives

1939 Ford Pickup
Excessive exposure to the sun is detrimental to the skin, both human and steel, as witness this bleached and wrinkled pickup formerly known as a Ford. Baking for way too many tanning seasons in the hot, unrelenting sun of western Colorado, the number of usable parts remaining on this dried-out Blue Oval carcass is now down to two: the rear fender strap and the spare tire holder. As for the front fender. . . .

Clipper

Bob Johnson's Auto Literature Archives

1956 Packard Clipper
Dry docked for about an eternity, this classy Clipper ship's sailing days are over. As it waits in the warm west central California sun for someone to come forth and make it roadworthy once again, it sits as a nostalgic reminder of everything that was good about the fabulous fifties. From its bullet bumpers and hooded lights to its Miami-inspired pastel green and white color scheme, it still offers big-car value at medium-collector-car cost.

Photo by Edward Burchard

Photo by Edy Rayfield

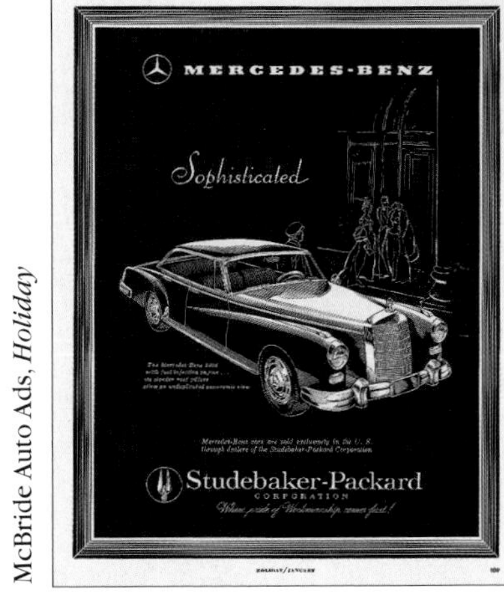

McBride Auto Ads, *Holiday*

1958 Mercedes-Benz
The tell-tale sign of the collector-coveted California black plate shows that this former pride of Germany has been residing on the left coast since the sixties, if not before. It appears to have been sitting in this same spot since the sixties, too, judging by the enveloping growth of nasturtiums in its northern California location. With its imposing grille and fuel-injected 115-horsepower six, this 220SE may be restorable, but first it needs a serious clipping.

McBride Auto Ads, *Holiday*

Photo by Dennis Vanderpoel

McBride Auto Ads,

1958 DeSoto

Gobs and gobs of money would be needed today to restore this fabulous finned DeSoto to showroom-new condition—the help of these nine sailors wouldn't hurt, either. As it's been sitting in the damp earth of a Minnesota clearing for way too many years, one can only imagine the amount of fabrication needed to make the undercarriage solid once more. Still, its durable 361-cubic-inch Turboflash V8 might need only a little help to make it rev once more.

1957 Chevrolet

Apparently the owner of this once very popular Chevrolet sedan wasn't sufficiently proud of his fancy fifties dream machine, so he thoughtlessly abandoned it in a picturesque field somewhere in western Connecticut. With a body that appears solid and straight, this muscular beauty can easily be restored thanks to the loyal support of many aftermarket parts manufacturers.

Photo by Dennis David

DODGE

McBride Auto Ads, *The Literary Digest*

1920s Dodge
The business of moving used furniture in overload-mode must have been just a little too tough for this 1920s-era Dodge truck to handle. Left to its own devices on the side of a back road in Minnesota, its paint has aged to a pleasing patina, complementing quite nicely the weathered wooden chairs atop its roof. With a pair of logs carefully positioned to protect it from passing vehicles, it appears it may eventually be in business once again.

Photo by G.Alan Nelson

Photo by Bill Magers

THE
NEW FORD
V-8 CYLINDER
CAR

Bob Johnson's Auto Literature Archives

1932 Ford Coupe
A valiant rodder's attempt to turn yet another '32 Ford into a race car has been clearly abandoned alongside a barn in southwestern Iowa. Judging by the poor fit of its homemade sheetmetal hood, the combination of too little cash and two left hands are the most probable causes. But it still has potential, with its wide wheels and fat tires giving it a nice stance. And look how its in-vogue distressed paint finish lends it a very "contemporary" appeal.

Cadillac

Where Craftsmanship is a Creed!

McBride Auto Ads, *Saturday Evening Post*

1960 Cadillac
Show us a person who lives in a pink house and we'll show you a person who drives a pink Cadillac, both of which, in this case, just happen to be located in the "Show Me" state of Missouri. With snow covering the trunk lid, the shape and size of the finned quarters are clearly defined, making clear that body repair and repaint on this former Kansas City cruiser would be a labor-intensive job considering its football-field-size dimensions. It's the kind of project that only a skilled craftsman can execute properly.

Photo by Martin Zehr

Photo by Gerald Jendrusch

Knowledgeable people buy Imperial

-and they buy it by the case

McBride Auto Ads,

1959 BMW Isetta
How strange that this example of one of the smallest cars ever made was found in the state where everything is big—Texas! Was its abandonment prompted by its small size, or did those homemade front "hood scoops" cause speed-reducing drag to the point where one could walk faster? Most probably it's the lack of much-needed air conditioning and the severely limited carrying space of this Bavarian pretzel compared to the ever-popular "Texas Cadillac"—a Suburban.

THE COUNTRY GENTLEMAN

May, 1929

Good performance with economy

O'Brien's Auto Ads

Photo by Tony Doughty

1928 Ford Model A
A 1928 Fordor sedan, obviously down on its luck, weathers a snowstorm in southern Vermont. With 3,572,610 Model As manufactured by Ford from 1927 to 1931, their solid construction and durable 40-horsepower L-head four-cylinder engines made them reliable transportation for those living in the rural countryside, (excepting, of course, for this particular Vermont owner). Pounded by snow for years, this car still remains in a restorable state.

Photo by Jim Howe

Discovered! The Biggest Low Priced Car of all time!

Recently published analysis of four leading low priced cars reveals these amazing facts

TERRAPLANE

$595

McBride Auto Ads,

1936 Hudson Terraplane
The distinguishing grille hibernating under a blanket of freshly fallen snow in a north central Minnesota salvage yard can be none other than that of a Terraplane. Aerodynamic by design, its sleek shape and exclusive Radial Safety Control suspension made it a hit with buyers who know quality when they see it. As the debonair man in the ad says, "It's the biggest money's worth I ever saw!"

McBride Auto Ads, *Better Homes & Gardens*

1946 Ford
The crystal ball looked rosy for returning GIs in the post-war era, with well-built affordable cars such as this 1946 Ford coupe available. Thanks to their sturdy construction, they aren't too hard to find today, but you'll want one with its front-end still attached. Appearing to be an abandoned project, this "half" Ford quietly awaits warmer days in northwest Georgia. With the front-end MIA, another peek into the crystal ball would be required to see whether it was originally powered by the 90-horsepower straight-six or 100-horsepower L-head V8.

Photo by Bob Baker

Photo by Lucia Beeler

McBride Auto Ads,

1948 Buick
Down on its luck, this hen-pecked Buick Roadmaster sits among a flock of fine feathered friends on a friendly family farm in the colorful bluegrass country of central Kentucky. The tasty little chickens, oblivious that Mother Nature is transforming the once-proud comely flanks of that big hulk of a Buick into the same earthy brown color as them, feed quietly now that the 144-horsepower, 320-cubic inch V8 sits silent.

CORVAI

McBride Auto Ads

1964 Corvair
At any reasonable speed, most any Corvair is at least marginally safe to drive. Unfortunately, this frugal little two-door isn't one of them, due to its lengthy sojourn in the woods of Puget Sound, hiding from someone named Ralph! With a severely oxidized body and an engine frozen solid as a rock, years of hard work and lots of swap meet searching lie ahead for the Chevrolet enthusiast determined to make it purr again. But in the end, the hugs of rewards will be worth the squeeze on your bank account.

Photo by Kimball Andrew Schmidt

Photo by Peter Romanchuk

'30 Willys sales literature didn't surface. We're still looking.

1930 Willys
Looking a little disheveled from sitting too many years in a thicket in British Columbia's damp woods, this six-cylinder 1930 Willys remains in relatively solid condition, a testimony to its outstanding build quality. It appears complete and ready to hit the road, with license plate still attached and hardened tires full of air, but a quick check of the 19-inch wheels is in order to ensure that termites haven't weakened the wooden spokes.

McBride Auto Ads, *Saturday Evening Post*

1940 Buick
General Motors was so proud when Mr. Best purchased one of their Buick V8s that they had to tell the world all about it. Some of the features Mr. Best must have liked were the "Micropoised Dynaflash" valve-in-head straight-eight engine, "Catwalk-cooling," "Buicoil" springing for a "Full Float" ride, and "tiptoe" hydraulic brakes. Abandonment of this pre-war gem in the central Maine woods may have resulted from the owner's inability to understand the General's unique language when reading the operator's handbook.

Photo by Gary Langley

Photo by Andy High

Take a Ride across these pages .. and then across town in the *NEW 1936 CHEVROLET*

One ride and you'll never be satisfied until you own
The only complete low-priced car

McBride Auto Ads, *Saturday Evening Post*

1936 Chevrolet
No more rides across town for this classy looking pre-war Chevrolet sedan. As it withers away in a Michigan field, young evergreens have grown up around it, protecting it against the cold winter winds from the north. The body remains straight and sound despite its disheveled appearance. It's missing the three Ws—windows, wheels, and water pump—but a quick search of the classified ads on www.hemmings.com is all that's needed to find the necessary parts.

McBride Auto Ads, *Time Magazine*

1937 Chrysler
Style! Power! Room! Value!
It looks as though this Chrysler Royal, languishing in the woods of southwestern Connecticut, still retains those salesworthy characteristics. From its insulated steel body to the Gold Seal engine that returns up to 24 miles per gallon, its noteworthy features are many. Amazingly, it cost only $810 brand new; just a tad more than it might cost today to buy it, have it pulled from its current resting place and flat-bedded a few miles to your favorite restoration shop.

Photo by Art Anderson

Photo by Jerry Reisinger

1960 Simca Elysee
The benefits of costing a mere penny a mile to operate, as claimed in the ad, just weren't enough incentive to keep this cute-looking French sedan from being used as a tree retreat instead. If you stay awake nights dreaming about restoring old Simcas, a trip down-under would be required to retrieve this Gallic wonder from a desolate New Zealand pasture. Chrysler's reason for giving up importing these little Parisians into the States was no mystery—today the mystery is the whereabouts of the Elysee's 50-horsepower four-cylinder engine.

In Paris a gallon of gas costs 74¢ Twice as much as it costs in the U.S.—so Frenchmen have to make it go twice as far. That's why so many of them drive Simcas. What mileage does Simca get over here? To find out, a stock Simca made ten test runs between twenty American cities—all under actual day-to-day driving conditions. The final average, certified by the U.S. Auto Club 38.058 mpg. Or less than 1¢ a mile for gasoline. (And in straight city driving, Simca averaged over 33 mpg.) Take a look at the Simca above. Ever see a nicer way to save money?

SIMCA imported by CHRYSLER priced at $1698*

McBride Auto Ads

McBride Auto Ads, *The Literary Digest*

90 The Literary Digest for March 16, 1929

for Economical Transportation

The Literary Digest for March 16, 1929 91

Better than 20 Miles *to the* Gallon!

Of all the performance qualities which make the new Chevrolet Six an outstanding achievement in advanced design, none is creating more wide-spread comment and approval than its ability to deliver better than twenty miles to the gallon of gasoline.

Such economy of operation would be unusual in *any* automobile. But in the new Chevrolet it is literally amazing! For here it is combined with all the superiorities of six-cylinder performance—tremendous reserve power, thrilling speed, flashing acceleration and marvelous six-cylinder smoothness.

When the new Chevrolet six-cylinder motor was in the first stages of development years ago, Chevrolet and General Motors engineers regarded fuel-economy as a factor of vital importance.

Over one hundred different motors were designed and tested during a period of four years. And the present power plant was approved and adopted only after it had displayed an all-round performance unapproached in any other low-priced car . . . and had clearly demonstrated its ability to operate so economically that anyone who could afford an automobile could afford to own and operate a Chevrolet Six!

This remarkable fuel-economy has been achieved by utilizing numerous engineering advancements, such as non-detonating high-compression cylinder head, hot spot manifold, acceleration pump and semi-automatic spark control.

Visit your Chevrolet dealer and inspect the beautiful new Fisher bodies. Ask for a demonstration. Learn by actual experience how masterfully this great new automobile handles in traffic—how easily it sweeps up the steepest hill—how quietly and smoothly it maintains full throttle speed for hour after hour over any road in perfect comfort. And as you drive, remember that it re-emphasizes Chevrolet's fundamental policy expressed in the famous Chevrolet slogan "For Economical Transportation."

CHEVROLET MOTOR COMPANY, DETROIT, MICHIGAN

Division of General Motors Corporation

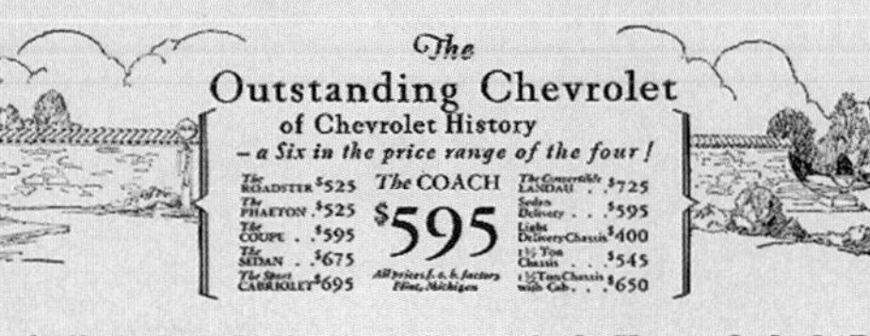

1929 Chevrolets
In the state of speed limits pushing triple digits, these two Chevys are pushing up daisies instead. No longer able to harness the power of their 46 horses, they lazily graze on a north central Montana prairie, indifferent to the world around them. Yet, their intrinsic GM quality remains, as evidenced by the restorable condition of their straight steel bodies. While the topless model (no pun intended) needs a little extra loving care, at least its radiator grille still shines bright.

Photo by Cat McKeen

Photo by Bob Prevallet

O'Brien's Auto Ads, *Saturday Evening Post*

1947 Dodge
Whatever caused the owners of this lovely looking farm in South Dakota to desert both their house and car will never be known. What we do know is that it'll take the better part of a lifetime to restore the original beauty of either or both, as well as a lottery windfall, 28,002 aspirins, 5 tetanus shots, 347 band-aids, and about four-thousand cases of beer. Not to mention the assistance of the entire state of Rhode Island. And that's just to start.

McBride Auto Ads, *Saturday Evening Post*

1947 Chevrolet Fleetline Aerosedan
Smart buyers will look elsewhere for an old car to restore. Although it's relatively solid and rust-free, frustrated hunters roaming the canyons of southern Utah have bullet-riddled the body of this sleekly designed Aerosedan, meaning years of parts searching and panel beating for anyone interested in resurrecting it. While its 90-horsepower straight-six is still there, the missing door trim, hood, and many other parts will probably discourage most potential buyers from rescuing it.

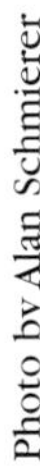
Photo by Alan Schmierer

Photo by Bob McClellan

The one in the middle isn't afraid of the dark.

SAAB

McBride Auto Ads

1967 Saab 96
Many Americans were afraid of early Saabs due to their unconventional engineering and oddball styling. Many still are. Perhaps the owner of this 1967 Saab 96 felt the same way when he abandoned his little Swedish meatball in the woods of South Carolina. As far as restoration projects go, its straight, rust-free shell will make it a breeze to restore (at least until it's time to rebuild its unique 46-horsepower, two-stroke, inline three-cylinder engine).

McBride Auto Ads

Photo by Rachel Naske

1953 Packard Clipper
According to our intrepid photographer, some farmer took the saying, "Necessity is the mother of invention," seriously when he transformed his old Clipper into something more useful to him than mere comfortable transportation: He turned it into a facility to store chicken feed! Makes no sense. Especially considering its restorable if slightly "hen pecked" condition. So here it sits, on a southeastern Pennsylvania farm, helping to make thousands of future fryers fat.

McBride Auto Ads

1950 Lincoln
Nothing would be finer than to than to see this shapely four-door Lincoln sedan restored to its former elegance. With a body that appears to have withstood the rigors of east Texas's climate, mechanical problems must have been why its owner parked it and forgot it. More than likely the 336-cubic-inch V8 wasn't the cause, as they are highly understressed engines and very durable. If ever there was an excellent candidate for a ground-up restoration, this Lincoln would be it.

Photo by Jon Paul Bordovsky

Lady-make up your (HUSBAND'S) mind!

$795

You'll be Happier in a NASH

McBride Auto Ads. *Life Magazine*

1940 Nash
Somebody's mind was made up to dump this neat Nash in a sea of fine friendly ferns somewhere in New York State's Catskill mountains. Like area native Rip Van Winkle, its twenty-year snooze under a tree has put it out of touch with the present and just about beyond hope. Why the driver's side grille assembly was removed, then placed atop the fender, is one of life's little mysteries, just like the reason for its being driven into the woods in the first place.

Photo by Jennifer Selib

Photo by Brian Larson

McBride Auto Ads. *The Literary Digest*

1932 Packard Light Eight
We wish we could ask the man who owned this stunningly beautiful pre-war Packard why he abandoned it in the woods of central Alabama. Did it run out of gas? Bend an axle? Or did he just lose his mind? We'll never know. But we do know that this classic gem is worthy of a second chance, since production of this remarkable coupe was very limited. Its 110-horsepower straight-eight engine and silent synchro-mesh transmission made it a pleasure to drive about town in its day. May its day come again!

Photo by Tom Narwid ©

McBride Auto Ads

1966 Dodge Coronet
A rebel without a cause and a forgotten example of one of the most desirable muscle machines of all time, this 383-powered Coronet 500 is now planted at a farm in Vermont's "Northeast Kingdom." No longer swingin' in style, its combination of chiseled good looks and tire-smoking power makes it hard for Mopar fans to resist its appeal, especially when it can graffiti the streets with black stripes at a rebellious throttle-stomp's notice.

Photo by William T. Randol

McBride Auto Ads

1951 Henry J
A Gold Medal is exactly what you deserve if you can make this peculiar-looking Henry J perform like the day it was built. The telltale signs of body repair gone astray hint that someone once tried to revive it, but to no avail. Sitting in the dry climate of New Mexico, it should remain relatively rust-free for years to come, 'til that eventful day when a dedicated enthusiast, up for the restoration challenge, will make its 68-horsepower Willys-Overland four-cylinder purr once more.

BIG SKY COUNTRY
49-1908

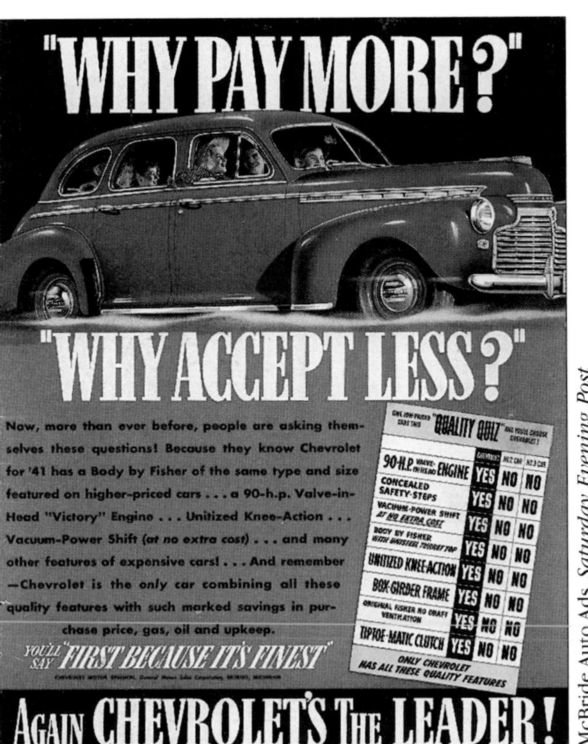

McBride Auto Ads, *Saturday Evening Post*

1941 & 1931 Chevrolets
This pair of Bowtie buddies keep each other company in an isolated setting behind a dilapidated building in central Montana. Although abandoned, they're still aesthetically pleasing to the eye, and with all their original trim still intact, they appear to be easy cars to restore. Thanks to the dry "Big Sky Country" climate, projects like these are worth pursuing in lieu of higher priced northeastern rust buckets. After all, why pay more?

Photo by Daniel Wesen

Photo by Robert Harmon

DON'T LET OTHERS *Spoil Your Fun!*

It's that New NASH

McBride Auto Ads, *Colliers*

1939 Nash
If you appreciate the rustic patina of abandoned cars, as well as the sport of climbing rocks, then don't let others spoil the fun of enjoying both hobbies at the same time. Here in the arid hills of eastern Utah, lies the car that everybody likes, a pre-war Nash sedan. But bring plenty of rope to get a closer look, as it is resting halfway up the side of this rocky mountain. Boy, those old Nashes, they go everywhere!

CHEVROLET FOR 1939

MASTER DE LUXE TOWN SEDAN

MASTER DE LUXE SPORT SEDAN

MASTER DE LUXE FOUR-PASSENGER COUPE

MASTER DE LUXE BUSINESS COUPE

MASTER DE LUXE COACH

MASTER DE LUXE SEDAN

Bob Johnson's Auto Literature Archives

1939 Chevrolet Woody and Coupe, 1950 Studebaker Convertible, and 1935 Ford Convertible
The always-damp climate of Georgia's Cumberland Island has wreaked havoc on this once-proud stable of American thoroughbreds, which are now rotted beyond the point of providing even a smidgen of worthwhile parts. With their broken bodies, rotted wood, frozen engines, rusted metal, cracked glass and pitted chrome, they bring new meaning to that overused old car hobby phrase: "Needs Work."

Photo by Mike Day

Photo by Sherri Martin

1937 Chevrolet
This Chevrolet two-door sedan stands guard over a ghost town somewhere in the high hills of southern California. Clearly past its prime, the Chevy's chiseled good looks haven't deteriorated nearly as fast as its abandoned cousins in the northeast, thanks to the dry southwest climate. Though many parts are missing in action, we remain hopeful that its new-for-'37 "Diamond Crown" styling can still be restored to the glory of its former self.

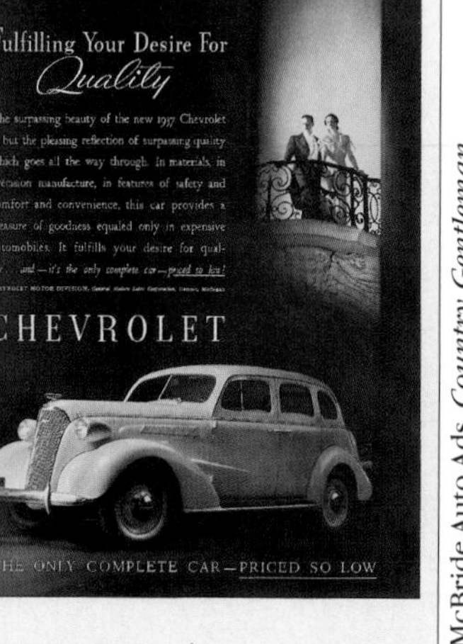

McBride Auto Ads, *Country Gentleman*

McBride Auto Ads, *The American Magazine*

1941 Plymouth and 1947 Dodge
Mopar buddies through and through, a rusty pre-war Plymouth sits beside its younger post-war Dodge cousin under a dramatic sky in Northern Idaho. Proudly wearing its Washington license plate, the shiny black Dodge appears to be the better of the two. Yet both classy Chrysler products require a heavy-duty wrecker's assistance to pull them out of this bumper-deep field of overgrown hay and into the garage of a Mopar enthusiast with lots of free time on his or her hands.

Photo by Colleen Hesson

Photo by Gillian Ehrich

Bob Johnson's Auto Literature Archives

1941 Plymouth
Treat yourself to the ultimate Mopar restoration project! What better starting point for building a new/old pre-war Plymouth could one ask for than this impressive stainless steel grille gleaming in the hot southern Utah desert? With a little bondo to plug the bullet holes in the doors, a new fender or two, and a few windows, you could soon be on your merry way. Of course, that's if the highly durable engine that made Plymouth famous is still in there.

DODGE
ZZB 715
WASHINGTON

Bob Johnson's Auto Literature Archives

1957 Ford

It appears that somebody bushwhacked a path through these thorny woods of northeastern Vermont to assess the value of this forgotten fragmented fatigued forlorn four-door Ford. With its original 190-horsepower, 272-cubic-inch V8 replaced by a bush that isn't nearly as effective, it's no wonder this fifties classic hasn't been rescued. As it sinks deeper into the soil with each passing day, hope for a restoration is fading fast.

Photo by Jim Howe

O'Brien's Auto Ads, *Colliers*

1938 Ford Truck

Either this one-and-a-half-ton Ford truck is sinking into the ground or fallen leaves have piled up around it. Actually, it appears to be a combination of the two, due to its lengthy residence in the beech-filled woods of southern Vermont. As a green Green Mountain relic it appears to be in decent shape, especially its 1938-model-year-only medallion-less grille. Even the factory-equipped driver's side door mirror and about 15% of the front bumper chrome are still intact.

Photo by Tom Narwid ©

Photo by Chris Montgomery

McBride Auto Ads

1949 Cadillac
Cadillac made its great stylistic leap forward in 1948 with finned rear fenders and an all-new look. For 1949, the new OHV V8 was added to complement the modern styling. Today, this fastback still retains its sleek looks, even while sinking into the sands of a New Mexico junkyard—a far cry from the distinguished-looking advertising cleverly displaying the famous Cadillac V in the form of dazzling jewelry.

Photo by Alan Schmierer

ALL-TRUCK *and Loaded With Power*

INTERNATIONAL *Trucks*

McBride Auto Ads, *Saturday Evening Post*

1946 International Pickup
Judging by his thumbs-up approval and positive disposition, Mr. Jones seems to be real happy with his International pickup. And rightly so, as it was loaded with lots of power thanks to its famous Green Diamond engine. Popular with home builders throughout the forties and early fifties, this sad looking pickup, abandoned on a farm in south central Utah, is in desperate need of a little remodeling itself.

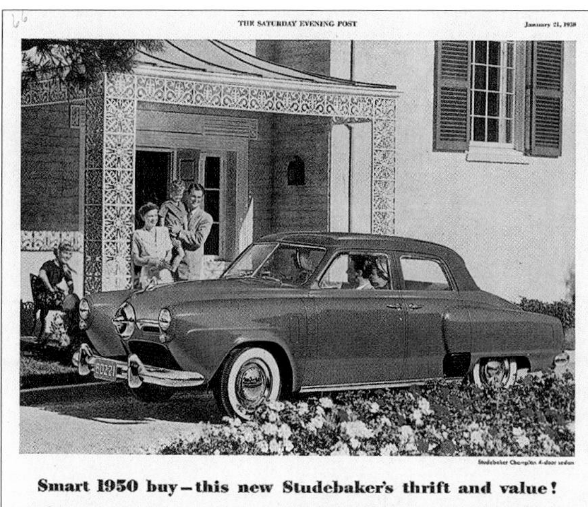

McBride Auto Ads, *Saturday Evening Post*

1950 Studebaker
While this bullet-nosed Studebaker may have been a smart buy in 1950, it would hardly be a thrifty value today, due to a body ravaged by Virginia creeper and the dreaded east coast tinworm. Lacking a few essentials such as a hood, wheels, tires, and its straight-six engine, it sits idly on a farm in central Michigan, perhaps the result of its owner's discontent with the brawny ball-shaped broadcasting beauty of its budding, bulky bullet nose.

Photo by Thomas V. McIntyre

Photo by J. D. Nelson

McBride Auto Ads

1967 Ford Mustang 2+2
The Chevrolet-inspired rendition of the word Ford—"Found on road dead"—rings too true for this muscle Mustang ditched on the side of a road in northeastern North Carolina, perhaps by a Camaro enthusiast. Judging by its dull red paint and rusted door, it's been sitting there for some too many years. Odd, since this model rates high on the lists of Mustang lovers everywhere.

Bob Johnson's Auto Literature Archives

1960 Metropolitan
Resting and rusting in a south central Connecticut junkyard, alongside fellow vehicular castaways of distinction, the red, white and blue weathered paint scheme looks very patriotic on this very un-American Metropolitan. By the standards of its day, it was a David in the land of finned Goliaths, which is why many ended up in this same un-loved state. Although its body is a real goner, the hardtop at least is worth salvaging.

Photo by Jeffrey Lepak

Photo by Wendell Blevins

Just Look What Low Price Buys!

PLYMOUTH BUILDS GREAT CARS

McBride Auto Ads

1939 Plymouth
What appears to be a body-off restoration project stopped mid-stream, the frame-less shell of this impressive looking Plymouth coupe is still salvageable despite its sojourn in this north central Ohio field. With its imposing grille and flowing front fenders, restoration to its once proud deco-inspired elegance is just a new frame and a half-ton of driveline and suspension parts away. Of course the price tag will be rather high.

"OUR NEW PLYMOUTH is Buying my Fall Clothes!"

Actually Saves 12% to 20% on Gasoline and Oil!

Only Plymouth gives you All Four:

1. GENUINE HYDRAULIC BRAKES
2. SAFETY-STEEL BODY
3. WEIGHT RE-DISTRIBUTION
4. 12% TO 20% LESS GAS & OIL

PLYMOUTH Now only $510

McBride Auto Ads, *Better Homes & Gardens*

1935 Plymouth
With a distinctively designed grille, it's a shame that this art deco-inspired body style was available one year only, thus making the task of restoring this derelict old Plymouth (abandoned in the bush somewhere in southwestern New Mexico) all the more challenging. All the glass and trim is missing, the interior's in shambles, and the 85-horsepower straight-six is not its complete self, but its safety-steel body is totally rust free, saving you money on welding repairs to buy your fall clothes!

Photo by Larry Bogel

Photo by Wendell Blevins

1949 Oldsmobile 88
After rocketing into its future, this Olds 88 burned up on re-entry and landed in a windswept field in northern Ohio. As its huge visor protects the windshield below, just like the covers over each headlight, the thick Body by Fisher sheetmetal has prevented this handsome-looking coupe from becoming just another parts car. With its Whirlaway Hydra-Matic transmission and high-compression Rocket V8, this is one post-war collectible with which someone should make a restoration date.

ANNOUNCING THE NEW "88" ANOTHER FUTURAMIC WITH NEW ROCKET ENGINE!

"The New Thrill" FUTURAMIC OLDSMOBILE

McBride Auto Ads, *Saturday Evening Post*

Ken W. Purdy writes on Porsche.

"... delivers more sheer sensual pleasure than anything else on wheels."

"The Porsche may be the most fun to drive of anything in the world," says sports car expert, Ken W. Purdy, writing in *Playboy*. "A great many authorities think so. One must fold and twist a bit to get into it. Once in, there's all the room in the world. The seats are contoured to reach around and hold you gently at the hips and shoulders. Visibility over the sloping nose is perfect. The gearshift lever moves as smoothly as a spoon of molasses, and you can slam it back and forth from gear to gear just as quickly as you can move your hand.

"The available acceleration of the Porsche is astounding; the brakes are about 50% oversize and air-cooled beyond any possibility of fade, and the steering, very soft and very quick, is what power steering tries to be and is not. The Porsche was designed for 50-50 fore-and-aft weight distribution. At about 60 miles an hour, air-pressure bears down on the wind-tunnel-bred frontal area and the balance becomes exact almost to a pound. There is virtually no wind-roar audible to a Porsche driver. He sits there . . . clipping through holes in the traffic-pattern that just aren't there for anybody else, and, when he wants to, running away from almost anything he sees. And the car is built. I've never heard a rattle in a Porsche. I've seen salesmen sit on the doors and swing back and forth. Why not? They have bank-vault hinges.

" . . . There will never be very many Porsches, since the factory is small, and they cannot be made quickly in any case. . . The competition models have a fabulous racing record, of course, and many American owners race the car. But its place in our scuderia is not as a competition car. It is included here because it delivers more sheer sensual pleasure than anything else on wheels. Driving a Porsche, you can, with small effort, believe that the seat of your trousers is a part of the automobile."

PORSCHE

EXPLORE YOUR OWN RESPONSE TO A PORSCHE. *Drive one today. Drive one every day for about $4200. For nearest dealer's name, write Porsche of America Corp., 107 Wren Avenue, Teaneck, N.J.*

McBride Auto Ads

1962 Porsche 356

How much sensual pleasure one can obtain from restoring this old Porsche depends upon how much one appreciates its characteristic rounded curves and inverted bathtub styling. Although it appears straight and complete, its having sunk into this central-Illinois lawn can mean only one thing: a very weak or rusted-through floor pan. But considering the 356's spirited performance and inspiring handling, the effort and expense might be well worth it.

Photo by Gary Brown

Photo by Thomas M. Healy

1923 Maxwell

This good Maxwell has been sadly forgotten in the woods of southern Maine. Most probably your local Pep Boys will not have a replacement hood and windshield frame in stock, but that shouldn't deter anyone from undertaking its rebuild; parts can still be discovered at the Hershey (Pennsylvania) AACA National Swap Meet each fall. Rarely seen at car shows today, Maxwells are quite sturdy with their 25-horsepower four-cylinder engines, and can take a lot of abuse.

McBride Auto Ads, *The Literary Digest*

THOMPSON
Phone WO 5-2366
Selma, N.C.

McBride Auto Ads

1948 Ford tow truck
After a laborious existence racing to the rescue of all sorts of vehicles crippled by accidents or mechanical gremlins, this rugged-looking Ford now deserves a little emotional rescue of its own. The encroaching vines of a farm in northeastern North Carolina aggressively try to hide its unsightly rust-covered body. If it weren't "Bonus Built," its demise would have taken place 19.6% of a lifetime ago.

Photo by Chris Montgomery

Photo by Mary Gibson

Bob Johnson's Auto Literature Archives

1953 Chevrolet
After a career of carrying surfers and surfboards down to the beach, this once rockin' Chevrolet Townsman station wagon is now an intrinsic component of someone's inventive side yard botanical display. Located near the Oakland waterfront on San Francisco Bay, the wagon's simulated wood-grain trim blends in naturally with the surrounding flora, adding a tad of welcome beauty to an otherwise typical industrial setting.

FORCES

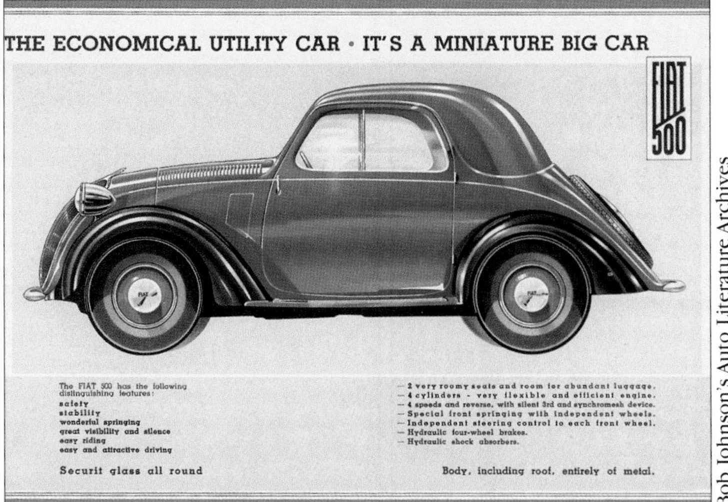

Bob Johnson's Auto Literature Archives

1937 Fiat
Born in Europe, lived in Africa, died in North America; the globe trotting status of this forgotten little Italian Fiat sedan is quite intriguing. Licensed by a U.S. Forces serviceman years ago in Ethiopia, it now enjoys a quiet, sunny retirement in the dry climate of north central New Mexico. A rare sight on American roads, pre-war Fiats were well built automobiles with thicker metal than their younger siblings. But just like their younger brethren, Americans found them not very desirable.

Photo by William T. Randol

Photo by Robert Harmon

WHAT 1939 CAR IS PACKED WITH *New Ideas?*

TAKE A LOOK *—that's all Dodge asks!*

NEW LOW PRICES!

New 1939 DODGE *Luxury Liner*

McBride Auto Ads

1939 Dodge
A knowledgeable mind packed with creative ideas is sorely needed to instill new life in this discarded dull dilapidated Dodge dumped in a field somewhere in southwestern Colorado. With its once beautiful body banged, bruised and beaten into submission, many days of hammer and dolly use would be invested before approving looks are cast its way once again.

MP 634

Bob Johnson's Auto Literature Archives

1950 Chevrolet
Precariously perched atop notoriously weak concrete blocks, this restorable Chevrolet sedan is an accident waiting to happen. A set of heavy-duty jack stands to prevent injury or death is a must, along with some welding, fresh paint, rechromed bumperettes and matching tires. Hope springs eternal that this fine old Chevy, sitting alongside an abandoned building in Connecticut, doesn't suffer the same fate.

Photo by Jean Constantine

Photo by Catherine Resch

September, 1930 Country Life

FREE WHEELING! *The sensation of 1930!*
Studebaker's epochal contribution to motoring

The World Champion PRESIDENT · · *The World Famous* COMMANDER

McBride Auto Ads, *Country Life*

1930 Studebaker
Take on the resurrection of this pre-war Studebaker Dictator 6's scant remains, now sinking into the earth of central Vermont, and you too will be free wheeling . . . into bankruptcy! Your epochal contribution to the old car hobby will help relieve many swap meet vendors of numerous body, mechanical, electrical, trim and interior parts they've been lugging from meet to meet for years.

PIONEER SALOON

McBride Auto Ads

1952 Cadillac
What appears at first glance to be nothing more than a parts car is actually a very solid Cadillac begging for a much-needed restoration. Basking in the dry Nevada sun, its 190-horsepower, 331-cubic-inch V8 appears to be in its correct place, as do the Yugo-sized half-ton bumpers. Marking Cadillac's 50th Anniversary, it once sported special gold-finished castings for the V-shaped hood and deck emblems, which were probably hocked in desperation for gambling money.

Photo by Gordon Schilling

Photo by Jim Howe

O'Brien's Auto Ads

1969(?) Volkswagen Beetle
Sitting beside a well preserved barn in southwest Vermont, the object hidden beneath layers of freshly fallen snow appears to be none other than a Volkswagen Beetle. After all, are there any other vehicles blessed with the distinctive shape of a half-ball? While others may be a ball to drive, this Beetle is almost guaranteed to start, indifferent to its surrounding environment. Could this really be the shape of things to come?

The de Tomaso Pantera. Around $10,000.*

In Italy, men build cars with passion. One of them is Alejandro de Tomaso. And this is his car. Pantera. Conceived without compromise. A car so carefully built (it is virtually handmade) there will only be

2,500 made the first year. Mid-engined like a racing car. An ultra-high-performance sports coupe that stands a little higher than the average man's belt buckle, it seats two (and only two) and it's priced in the neighborhood of $10,000.

Obviously, Pantera is for the few who demand something extraordinary.

The body designed by the world-famous Ghia Studios—is Italian craftsmanship at its highest level. Monocoque construction fuses the steel skin and frame into an incredibly strong and rigid structure.

The engine is a 351 CID, 4-barrel V-8 placed just ahead of the rear axle, which gives Pantera some huge advantages over conventional sports cars. Better vision forward. Less power-loss. Better weight distribution. And the tightest, most satisfying handling characteristics you've ever experienced.

All this is standard: air-conditioning, five forward speeds fully synchronized, independent suspension of all four wheels, die-cast magnesium wheels, rack and pinion steering, power-boosted disc brakes—even an ingenious system to prevent you from inadvertently selecting the wrong gear while shifting. The de Tomaso Pantera

has to be one of the most impressive vehicles ever offered here at *any* price.

*Based on Manufacturer's suggested retail price. Excludes state and local taxes and destination charges.

Pantera by de Tomaso
Imported for
Lincoln-Mercury

To locate your nearest Pantera dealer, call free, any hour, any day 800-631-1971. In New Jersey, 800-962-2803.

LINCOLN • MERCURY

O'Brien's Auto Ads, *Motor Trend*

Photo by Lynda Hummel

10 Years of the lowest truck delivery expense you ever had!

3 DIVCO-TWIN Models for

DIVCO-TWIN TRUCK COMPANY • DETROIT

Divco-Twin

O'Brien's Auto Ads

Divco Delivery Truck
After a lifetime of delivering milk, butter, eggs and other dairy delectables for humans to sustain life, this well-designed Divco truck enjoys its retirement beneath the protective limbs of a giant red oak in central Michigan. It appears nearly fit for another round of early morning chores, and the enjoyable task of restoring its utilitarian beauty could probably be accomplished relatively easily.

1971 De Tomaso Pantera
Believe it or not folks, even exotic cars are foolishly discarded before their time. Somewhere in the woods of northwestern Connecticut, under an accumulating camouflage of dead foliage, rests this aggressive-looking Ghia-designed Pantera. Did its 351 Ford V8 engine submit to the pressures of excessive revs, or did its complex transaxle chip a tooth or two? Regardless, this chrome-bumper beauty deserves a better destiny.

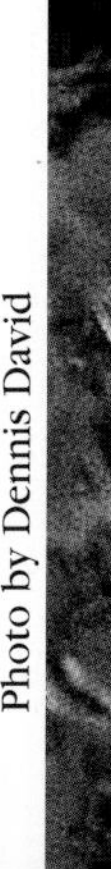

Photo by Dennis David

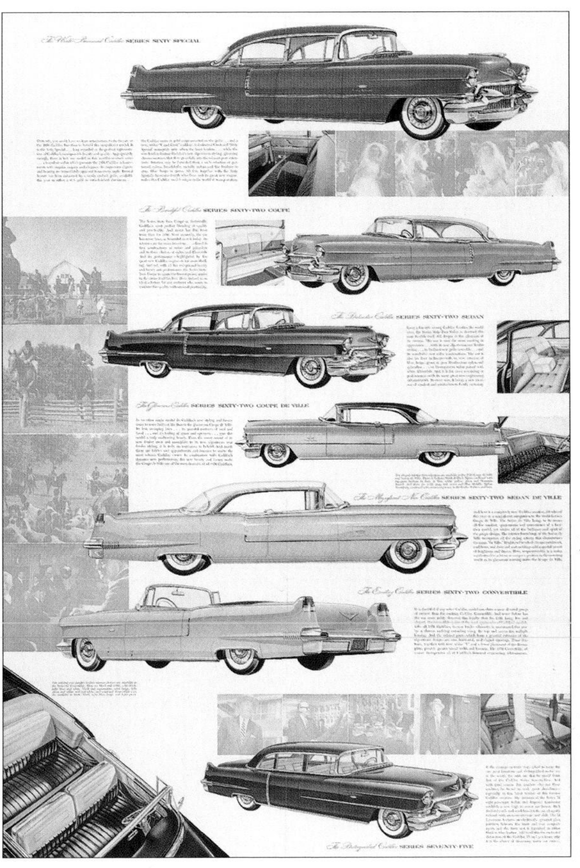

Bob Johnson's Auto Literature Archives

1956 Cadillac
Thanks to the huge Cadillac section of cars, parts, accessories and literature for sale each month in *Hemmings Motor News*, everything an enthusiast needs to restore the beauty of this Series 62 four-door sedan can be easily located. But first you'll have to roam the woods of Virginia to find the 4,430-pound behemoth. Let's hope someone gets there fast before the classy curvaceous Caddy sinks into oblivion.

Photo by Bill Randol

Photo by Robert C. Johnson

New Ford THUNDERBIRD

The most wanted, most admired car in America ...and it's priced far below other luxury cars!

ANOTHER FIRST FROM FORD

McBride Auto Ads, *Time Magazine*

1958 Ford Thunderbird
Ford's sporty two-seater evolved into a very different car in 1958 with the addition of a rear seat, bigger trunk, more spectacular styling and the obligatory-for-1958-cars quad headlamps. This downtrodden 'bird languishes in a Massachusetts field awaiting its fate as a donor car for another restoration—or perhaps it will be restored to its former flamboyant and powerful self, so it can cruise the coast once again.

Bob Johnson's Auto Literature Archives

1931 Model AA
Poison Parsnip has taken over Henry's handsome handicapped handiwork in the beautiful forest of Vermont's scenic "Northeast Kingdom." The faded glory of the black coachwork has been transformed by a none-too-pretty problematic powdery patina of rampant rough residue of runaway rust. The undented radiator grille makes a great starting point, however, for anyone up for the challenge of restoring this American icon.

Photo by Tom Narwid ©

Photo by Keith L. Mayne

McBride Auto Ads, *Saturday Evening Post*

Bob Johnson's Auto Literature Archives

1926 Hudson and Ford Model T
Resting beside each other like a pair of old drinking buddies working off a hangover, the Hudson sedan (left) appears far newer in design than the "chop top" Model T of the same vintage, a result, perhaps, of drinking a better grade of oil. Retired to a farm in central New York State, their oxidized state of disrepair has rendered them almost useless, save for a few body parts and one cut-off top.

O'Brien's Auto Ads

Photo by Purdy Conrad

"...NO LONGER A 'CAR WIDOW'"
Now I do go to town!
$495
BUY TWO NEW WILLYS FOR 1940

McBride Auto Ads

1940 Willys
Whether or not you'd want to be seen around town in this Willys four-door sedan is questionable. But thanks to the dry climate in Yakima, Washington, this rugged sedan remains in restorable condition. After some fresh paint, a pair of headlights, new side glass, and a hubcap or two, you could be styling down Main Street just like the happy lady behind the wheel in the ad, albeit at slow speeds due to the limitations of its little 61-horsepower four-cylinder engine.

1941 Chrysler Business Coupe
Forgotten in a field somewhere in Colorado, this aggressively styled 1941 Chrysler coupe's thick metal has remained in solid, rust-free condition thanks to the mile-high dry climate. All it appears to need before it hits the "Rocky" roads once again is a fresh coat of vivid paint applied to its well proportioned body and a thorough polishing of the multi-piece grille and chrome-plated trim and hubcaps but a mechanical inspection might reveal other needs.

Photo by Robert Harmon

McBride Auto Ads

1939 Ford Tudor
Transforming this attractive Tudor into a winner at the concours should be a relatively easy task, since it's very straight, fairly solid, and (apart from the missing hubcaps) mostly complete—and that's half the battle towards creating a show-winning restoration. As it waits for the harsh Minnesota winter to pass, it appears to be resting on blocks, perhaps to prevent it from sinking into the soft farm soil. Considering Ford's fine engineering and robust dependability, the flathead V8 should have no problems firing up.

Photo by G. Alan Nelson

Photo by Mary Lanteigne

"TRUCK FARMING" doesn't always mean "GROWING VEGETABLES"

A GOOD many farmers have discovered that their farm work, regardless of what kind it is, gets a lot easier and more profitable when they buy a Ford V-8 Truck.

The reason is that the Ford Truck is really a farm implement—rugged and dependable in the field, fast and economical on the road. Unlike so many farm implements, it is never put away for the season. There is always work for it to do. In winter, equipped with power take-off, it grinds the feed and saws the wood. In the spring it is out in the fields hauling seed, fertilizer and tools. All through the harvest it is a time and labor saver. And all year round it is back and forth from farm to market.

In 1940 you're pretty sure to find the exact Ford V-8 Truck that can make this kind of "truck farming" a paying proposition for you. There are 42 body and chassis types, 6 wheelbases and a wide choice of special equipment.

No matter what size your farm, check the advantages of a Ford V-8 Truck by making an "on-the-job" test.

FORD V·8 TRUCKS

FORD MOTOR COMPANY, BUILDERS OF FORD V-8 AND MERCURY CARS, FORD TRUCKS, COMMERCIAL CARS, STATION WAGONS AND TRANSIT BUSES

O'Brien's Auto Ads, *Farm Journal*

1940 Ford Pickup
The rusted shell of this once admirable Ford pickup blends in perfectly with the yellows, oranges and reds of southern New Brunswick's colorful autumn foliage. In Canada, and across the globe, these versatile trucks were a commercial favorite, courtesy of their special combination of rugged construction quality, powerful V8 engines, and attractive styling. And just look at the durability of the hood ornament's chrome finish.

Buy a FORD and bank the difference

There's a new kind of value in the new kind of FORD

McBride Auto Ads, *Saturday Evening Post*

Photo by Dennis Neumann

1957 Ford
After sitting on the cold, windswept plains of North Dakota for what appears to be a dozen-plus years (judging by the size of the tree growing through its engine bay), it would take a vault-load of cash to restore the beauty of this fantastic Fairlane. But with its distinctive hooded headlights and Thunderbird-style fins, the expense would be worth it. Of course, if it were powered by a wood-burning stove, Mr. Tree would work fine, but a factory-original 272-cubic-inch V8 would develop a little more power.

Photo by Jeffrey Lepak

1958 Edsel
Forgotten in a central Connecticut graveyard for fifties-era automotive castaways, the stately elegance of this unsightly Edsel sedan still endures to beholders indifferent to its rust-scarred body. With its hallmark vertical "horse collar" grille and split bumper still in fine form, plenty of good usable parts remain to help other Edsels motivate the creative consciousness of future generations, even if Ford's Teletouch Drive doesn't push their buttons.

McBride Auto Ads

Bob Johnson's Auto Literature Archives

Photo by John Huffman

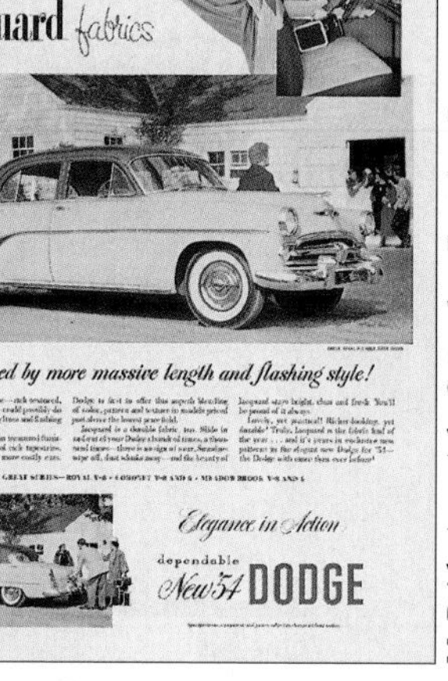

McBride Auto Ads, *Saturday Evening Post*

1954 Dodge Suburban
As a once proud elm tree fossilizes into legend on a central Ohio field, so, too, does this rarely seen eight-passenger two-door Dodge Suburban. With a production total of only 9,489 examples, it's a real shame that more of these pleasantly designed wagons, with their 110-horsepower straight-six engines, haven't been saved. Knock on wood, though, that the few Suburbans remaining shall be restored so the next generation of old car enthusiasts can admire them, too.

1941 Chevrolet Pickup
Nothing like owning an old truck that's never been hit! Judging by the straightness of the front bumper and complete chrome trim, this classy looking Chevy pickup may be the ideal restoration candidate. Naturally, due to its laborious career as a lobster trap hauler along the Maine coast, this stylish workhorse is long overdue for some fresh paint, not to mention an intense cleansing of its nose-numbing seafood aroma.

Photo by Tom Narwid ©

MAINE
974-97

Ufficio Tecnico Carr. Touring
dis. nº 1130 · dis. M.Vender

Design study courtesy of Carrozzeria Touring

1947 Alfa Romeo
How this ultra-rare coachbuilt Alfa immigrated to the cowboy country of central Texas will always remain a mystery. Thankfully the combination of the Lone Star State's dry climate and the Alfa's aluminum coachwork has preserved the body quite well, less, of course, a few dings and dents. Apparently a 6C 2500 Berlinetta, designed and fabricated by Carrozzeria Touring of Milan, this is one of only a handful made, making the restoration quite challenging.

Photo by Jim McWilliams

Photo by Leslie Miles

JAGUAR
Mark VII
Now with automatic transmission
THE FINEST CAR OF ITS CLASS IN THE WORLD

McBride Auto Ads

1953 Jaguar
Thanks to American engineering, Jaguar's early MK VII sedan sported an optional Borg-Warner automatic transmission for those lazy continental drivers who desired reliable comfort. Still, the troublesome Lucas electricals remained, which must have been the cause of this stately saloon's demise—that or the unavailability of British car parts in its hometown of Billings, Montana. Body repair on the front fender—oops, we meant wing!—is a positive sign for a rosy future, we hope.

Here you go in greatness

THE name is ROADMASTER—and you know why when you try its travel.

You sense immediately that you have the full power to handle whatever conditions your motoring may meet.

Miles seem to melt away—for every step of your way is through the absolute smoothness of Twin-Turbine Dynaflow.

Hills seem to humble before you — for the V8 engine you hold rein on can turn out the highest horsepower in all Buick history.

Curves seem to straighten out, dips and hollows seem to level off, bumps and ridges seem to velvet out — for here you travel in the industry's most envied ride, with coil springs on all *four* wheels, with torque-tube steadiness, with Safety Power Steering and a host of other engineering gems gentling the way.

And with all this — you go cloaked in the simple greatness of true style modernity, and every passer-by knows it.

Perhaps it is for these reasons that the Buick ROADMASTER this year is welcoming so many new owners to its membership.

For it is literal fact that ROADMASTER sales are soaring—that more and more people on the way up, as well as those long accustomed to fine-car ownership, are taking delivery of this bountiful Buick this year.

But add one more potent reason for this great success: ROADMASTER *is writing an impressive new record of economy with highly enviable gas-mileage figures.*

Why not see your Buick dealer for a demonstration? You have nothing to lose — and a great experience to gain. See him this week.

BUICK *Division of* GENERAL MOTORS

ROADMASTER *Custom Built by* BUICK

WHEN BETTER AUTOMOBILES ARE BUILT BUICK WILL BUILD THEM

McBride Auto Ads

Photo by Edward Burchard

1941 Studebaker

Clearly past its prime, this once-handsome 1941 Studebaker sedan has been rendered beyond the hopes and dreams of even the most talented of restorers by the ravages of time, Mother Nature and a few gun-toting cowboys. As it leisurely fossilizes into the south central red earth of New Mexico, it's losing even the capacity to donate serviceable parts, such as its 170-cubic-inch L-head inline six, so another Champion Custom Six could live on.

McBride Auto Ads, *Colliers*

1954 Buick

If you've ever pushed a two-ton-plus '54 Buick with three flats you'll understand why the owner of this grand Roadmaster is letting it flat-spot into eternity. Complete and virtually rust-free, thanks to its sabbatical in this dry Utah barn, this post-war collectible is a prime candidate for a thorough restoration. Behind that imposing chrome grille lies a 322-cubic-inch V8 that developed 200 horsepower at 4,000 rpm during its "We-like-Ike" youth.

Photo by Edward Burchard

EHA 921
UTAH 73

Index by Make